LEBRON JAMES

The Inside Story of How LeBron James Became King James of The Court

WHAT IT TAKES TO BE LIKE LEBRON

An Unauthorized Biography

By Steve James

"You can't be afraid to fail. It's the only way you succeed. You're not gonna succeed all the time, and I know that."

- LeBron James

TABLE OF CONTENTS

INTRODUCTION

LeBron James is 6 feet 8 inches tall and weighs 250 pounds. Most of his composition is pure muscle. He's big enough to be a ferocious and threatening power forward, but he can also handle the ball, shoot well from beyond the arc, and make needle-threading passes. Often referred to as an anomalous physical specimen, **LeBron James surely is someone that comes around once in a generation**.

LeBron has been under the spotlight since he was in high school. He was one of the most anticipated NBA draft picks of all time. And though no one else has come under the scrutiny that he has come under, he does not disappoint.

Spectators have had the opportunity to watch LeBron grow both on and off the court, since entering the NBA at 19 years old. **He has become one of the best players of today**, and possibly one of, if not the best, of all time.

Although the superstar now is one of the richest people in the world, he came from next to nothing, being moved around to various homes in the seediest parts of Akron, Ohio. He has created both a name for himself and for the city of Cleveland. And though he certainly possesses some natural and innate abilities, LeBron has spent countless hours over the course of his life focusing on specific goals, and doing anything possible to better his game.

In this book, we'll start from the beginning and progress through his life to see the changes he's made to become the Phenom he is considered to be today. We'll go through his high school years, and how he developed as a player and an athlete. We'll then cover how he transitioned to the NBA, and his improvement throughout his career – both on and off the court. We'll discuss the training he has done – in the gym, on the court, and mentally –

1

as we go into his psyche and understand **what it truly takes to be such a great athlete**. And finally, we'll learn about his philosophy of basketball, what motivates him to excel, and *find the takeaways that we can apply to our own lives*. This is LeBron James!

CHAPTER 1

UPBRINGING

Although LeBron James owns a 30,000 square foot house, which he bought at $9.2 million in Akron Ohio, this was hardly the world he grew up into. In fact, it was the polar opposite.

On December 30, 1984, LeBron James came into this world. His mother, Gloria James, was only 16 years old. And his biological father, Anthony McClelland, was an ex-convict who paid little attention to the family. As a result, LeBron took on his mother's last name and has kept it.

Gloria's mother died when LeBron was an infant. Naturally, for a 16-year-old with a child, no mother, and limited employment prospects, this was a difficult time. Struggling to maintain a sense of normalcy, the two moved around a lot within Akron. And with limited resources, Gloria remained committed to giving LeBron the best chance possible, keeping him away from violence and a life on the streets.

When LeBron was about two years old, Gloria began a relationship with Edie Jackson, who later went to prison in 1990 for cocaine trafficking. Despite his misdoings, he was instrumental in raising LeBron and assisting Gloria to look out for him.

However, when LeBron began going to school, the transition was difficult. Because he was constantly moving around and living a life quite different to many of his classmates, he struggled socially. **Sports became an outlet.** And these came in the form of basketball and football.

In basketball, he was a natural. **He looked up to Michael Jordan,** and mimicked his game to the best of his ability. In the fourth grade, in his first season playing football for the East Dragons, he scored 17 touchdowns in six games. Frankie Walker, his coach, saw the immense potential in his young athlete.

However, the same year, in the fourth grade, LeBron missed 82 out of 160 school days because of he and his mother's nomadic lifestyle. Additionally, Gloria spent 7 days in county jail throughout the year for committing petty crimes. Walker knew this would not be a sustainable lifestyle for someone so poised to become a great athlete. Walker spoke to Gloria about having LeBron move in with him and his family. While heartbroken to face the reality that she could not fully support her son, she, too, recognized it was the right thing to do, and *LeBron moved in with the Walkers.*

The transition was enormous. LeBron went from having a completely un-structured lifestyle to one full of structure. Frankie Walker had a wife Pam and three children. They were all responsible for upkeep of the house by doing daily chores. The following year, in the fifth grade, LeBron won the attendance award at school.

The next year LeBron moved back in with Gloria for a period of time. However, when it came to a point that she could not financially support both of them, he moved back in with the Walkers. Recognizing that the situation would become too difficult – LeBron living away from his mother – the Walker's opted to financially support Gloria and LeBron, assisting them with their rent and other expenses.

However, LeBron's time with the Walkers did not cease. One of the Walker boys with whom he lived – Frankie Jr. – and some other boys from the neighborhood, grew up playing basketball together, and challenged each other day in and day out. *Sian Cotton, Willie McGee, and LeBron James* would be the names people knew too well in the coming high school basketball championship years.

Dru Joyce II was an aspiring athlete in his early years. Having an influential coach in his early years, Dru Joyce II always wanted to give back to the sports community, but temporarily lost sight of that goal. However, he oversaw pickup basketball at his local church, and his son took a liking to the game. Then, he began coaching a travel basketball team, and a Salvation Army Board member arranged a place to practice for the children. Thus, the **Shooting Stars were born**.

LeBron was one of these players, and despite the hardships he was going through, he worked hard and kept up high spirits. The team travelled throughout Ohio and rarely lost. The boys all began playing together, and developing a chemistry that would last for years. They called themselves *"The Fab Four"* having sleepovers most weekends, and feeling like brothers to each other.

The team developed a dream to win a national championship. The dream began to become a reality when the team first qualified for the Amateur Athletic Union (AAU), which hosts national championships for all age groups. Because it is also where all of the college scouting occurs, it is the most competitive league before the NCAA in the United States. In the summer of 1999 the team dreamed to go to the national tournament but did not have sponsors or money. They tried fundraising themselves by selling fish fries, duct tape, washing cars, and were able to travel to Orlando, Florida in a few cars to see if they could make this dream a reality.

The Shooting Stars had far less experience than most of the teams in the tournament, which had played over 50 games. However, they persevered and continued advancing. This was when LeBron really began to shine. When they got to the championship game against the Southern California All-Stars who had won numerous years before, they were the clear underdogs. As half-time came, the Shooting Stars were down 45-30. However, with 1:30 left in the 4th quarter, the lead was narrowed to only 4 points. James scored a three-point play off of a magnificent drive and lowered the lead to 2 points. With 4 seconds left in the game LeBron was able to get off a decent three-point shot, but it bounced off the back of the rim and they lost the game.

However, not winning brought out something else in these boys. They realized they had unfinished business, and made a pact that they would all attend the same high school. Buchtel High School was essentially an all-black school and it was where most of these boys were expected to go.

There was pressure from the Black community to go to Buchtel, but because Dru Joyce III was small, and would not be given a chance to play ball there, they looked elsewhere. Keith Dambrot, the newly elected coach at St. Vincent-St. Mary High School saw potential in Joyce III. Thus, honoring their pact to stay together, all the boys decided to go to St. Vincent-St. Mary.

CHAPTER 2

HIGH SCHOOL YEARS

1999-2000 Season

Coach Keith Dambrot was on them from day one. He forced them to put their highest effort into every stretch, warm up drill, shooting effort, etc. And even **as freshman**, the group of young men was **playing at an unprecedented level of cohesiveness**.

In the first game of the season, a very nervous LeBron came out strong, scoring several breakaway layups. The next quarter, friends and teammate Dru Joyce III, often not taken seriously because of his 5'0" height and slight frame, stepped in, scoring an unbelievable 6 consecutive three-pointers. The Irish won the game 76-40, and LeBron finished with 15 points and 8 rebounds.

In their freshman season the boys went 27-0, and were being talked about widely in the press. LeBron averaged 21 points and 6 rebounds per game, leading the team to the Division III state title. In the semifinal LeBron scored 19 points and had 11 rebounds and in the championship game he put up 25 points. He was also named **MVP of the state tournament in Columbus**.

2000-2001 Season

As the boys entered their **sophomore year**, a new addition joined the team – Romeo Travis. However, Travis did not seamlessly mesh with the rest of the team. That said, the popularity and awareness that LeBron and this team were going places was unavoidable. They were not just winning; they were dominating.

The team even played at the University of Akron's Rhodes Arena to enable the amount of fans that wanted to attend to do so. The arena seated 5,492 seats, and fans, college, and even NBA scouts, began to fill those seats. The team was again successful, going 26-1 and winning the state championship. That season, LeBron averaged 25.2 points, 7.2 rebounds, 5.8 assists, and 3.8 steals per game. He was also named **Ohio's Mr. Basketball** and was **the first sophomore ever selected to the *USA Today* All-USA First Team**.

However, the immense success gave an opportunity to coach, Keith Dambrot. He was offered a college coaching position, and took it, much to the boys' dismay. Dru Joyce II, though initially hesitant, would become the new head coach.

2001-2002 Season

As LeBron and the Fighting Irish were entering their **junior year**, the stakes increased dramatically, as did the attention and the hype. The team would be competing on a national level, with an opportunity to take home the national title. Even before the season began LeBron was gaining national fame. He was featured in *SLAM Magazine* as "**the best high school player in America right now.**" Later during the season, he would become the first high school player to be the cover image for a *Sports Illustrated* issue.

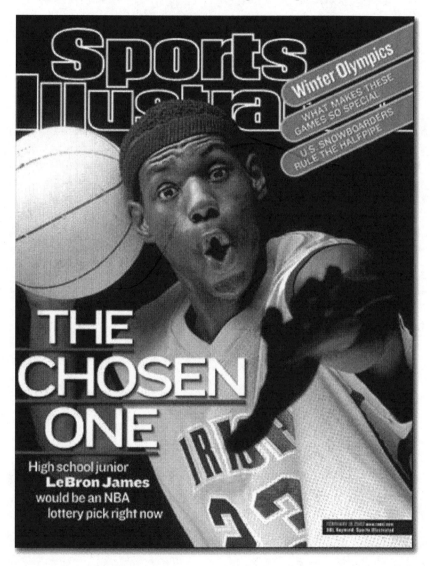

They opened the season in a dominating fashion, living up to much of the hype propagated by the media. It was clear that LeBron was becoming a sensation. Tickets were being scalped for over $200. The team received an Adidas sponsorship. Press, media, and young fans came to their hotels asking for autographs. It was... crazy.

As is often the case when 16 and 17 year olds get national attention, it goes to their head. Some of players began to neglect the coach's advice, and not take pre game rest and focus seriously. They arrived in the championship game playing in the packed Ohio State arena. Despite playing poorly, the Fighting Irish were able to keep the game close. With 22 seconds left, they trailed by 2. However, after missing a shot with 9 seconds left in the game, Dru Joyce III threw the ball against the rim, getting a technical foul. Two made free throws for the opposition and possession sealed the deal and the Irish lost the game.

The team ended with a record of 23-4, with a loss in the Division II championship game. LeBron finished the season with averages of 29 points, 8.3 rebounds, 5.7 assists, and 3.3. steals per game. Again he was named **Ohio's Mr. Basketball** and was selected to the *USA Today* **All-USA First Team**. He also won the *Gatorade National Player of the Year Award*. However, disappointment was all that was on LeBron's mind. In fact, he was so disappointed he considered petitioning to the NBA to allow him to enter the draft that year. He would later admit that he even smoked marijuana during this time.

2002-2003 Season

Entering their fourth and final season, the team made a conscious decision to approach the new year with a new attitude. Beginning in **July LeBron made a conscious effort to be a leader, and to win the championship**. They entered the season ranked 23 on the national level, but prepared to take on anyone.

In June 2002, before the season began, Coach Dru Joyce II called up *Speed Strength Systems*, a professional athletic training service, and asked if they would be willing to help out his team. Nene and J.R. Bremer were two

NBA prospects at the time, and the coach thought extra training would bring LeBron and the Fighting Irish's game to the next level. The details of this system and training exercises used are discussed at the end of this chapter.

After a summer with this serious training, the St. Vincent-St. Mary's team was more ready than ever, and their schedule was jam-packed. They even played a nationally televised game on ESPN2 against Oak Hill Academy – a school known to be a basketball academy and the top-ranked basketball team in the country. Dick Vitale and Bill Walton came in to commentate the game. The Irish came out chanting "We ready," to prove that they were a different and more composed team than the previous year. They won the game and proved that they were a real national threat. Time Warner Cable saw the potential economic benefits, and then offered the high school games with pay-per-view fees.

They played Strawberry Mansion in Philadelphia – who had the best team in Pennsylvania and the best scorer in high school basketball – and they beat them by a considerable margin. They blew out teams ranked much higher than them who were the best in their respective states.

The Fighting Irish faced the Mater Dei Monarchs with the stakes of taking the number one national ranking. Further, they were essentially the same team that the same group of boys had lost to in the AAU championship many years earlier. The stakes were particularly high. St. Vincent-St. Mary won the game, their 8th game, which was their 3rd win over a top-ten team. They instantly moved to the top of the rankings.

The school and the city of Akron were completely invested in this young team. However, **not all of the press was positive**. What came under particular and intense scrutiny was when his mother, Gloria, bought him a Hummer for his 18th birthday. Gloria was granted a loan, with the expectation that she would be able to pay it back easily, but for a kid who grew up in poverty, people relentlessly criticized LeBron and his mother. The Ohio High School Athletic Association (OHSAA) investigated the situation and determined that LeBron's acceptance of retro jerseys worth $845 from a clothing store, in exchange for being photographed, **made LeBron ineligible for the remainder of the season**. He still went to practice, but had to sit on the sideline, watching his teammates in despair.

LeBron sat on the bench in a suit in St. Vincent-St. Mary's first game without him. Though they adjusted, having to play a game without their superstar, they felt they had a lot to prove both for themselves and for LeBron.

They would end up winning 63-62.

Though still devastated, after watching from the sidelines he realized he needed to end up back on the court. He ended up appealing the decision, and after a two-game suspension, he was allowed to play the rest of the season. They had to forfeit one game of the season as a result, which ended up being their only loss.

James returned to the court and made a statement, **scoring a career-high 52 points**.

However bigger things were on his mind: winning a national championship with this same group of guys was conceived of in the 5th grade. Now, 9 years later, the challenge came in the same Ohio State arena as the previous year. The first play of the game LeBron threw down a two-handed slam-dunk.

The opposing team, Alter, countered by slowing down the game, and it worked considerably well. They went into the locker room after the first half losing the game. But the Irish fought back in the second half and ended up **winning their long-sought after national championship**.

James finished the season averaging 31.6 points, 9.6 rebounds, 4.6 assists, and 3.4 steals per game. Again, he was named **Ohio's Mr. Basketball**, *USA Today* **All-USA First Team**, and the **Gatorade National Player of the year**. He also participated in three different all-star games after the season. These included the EA Sports Roundball Classic, the Jordan Capital

Classic, and the 2003 McDonald's All-American Game. **Because he accepted free sports jerseys, he became ineligible to play in the NCAA.** It was then made official that he would enter the 2003 NBA draft, considered to be the "most hyped basketball player ever."

SPEED STRENGTH SYSTEMS

Before the beginning of 2002-2003 season, three days a week LeBron and his teammates did a range of both on and off court exercises to strengthen jumping muscles, strengthen shooting muscles, and do basketball-specific cardiovascular activities. Here was their three-day per week routine:

MONDAY

Power Plate Warm-Up Protocol

- *30 sec. Quarter Squat (35 Light)*: Stand with your feet shoulder-hip width apart with the knees slightly bent. Now dip down to a quarter squat position and hold for 30 seconds.

- *30 sec. Quarter Squat (35 Heavy) (invert and evert ankles)*: Maintaining a quarter squat position, invert your ankles and hold the position for 30 seconds then evert your ankles and hold for 30 seconds.
- *30 sec. Toe Touch (35 Light)*: Stand with your feet together and knees slightly bent. Now bend down and touch your toes.

- *30 sec. Full Squats (35 Heavy)*: Stand with your feet shoulder-hip width apart with the knees slightly bent. Now lower yourself to a parallel squat position (thighs parallel to the ground) and hold for 30 seconds.

Resistance Training

- *Bear Crawls with sled*: Get down on all fours with the sled's harness straps around your shoulders. Bear Crawl for 2 sets of 20 yards.

- *SSS Warm-up (3 Dead Lifts, 3 Hang Shrugs, 3 Hang Cleans, 3 Split Jerks)*: Complete the above exercises in a sequence switching exercises every 3 reps for a total of 12 reps.

- *Hang Cleans* –x5–x5–x5–x3

- *Hang Shrugs* –x3–x3–x3–x3
- *Bench Press* –x10–x10–x8–x8

- *Hammer Strength Reverse Grip Pulldowns* –x10–x10–x10: Use a reverse grip (palms facing inwards) on the Hammer Strength pulldown machine.

- *Single-Arm Dumbbell Incline Bench* –x8–x8–x8: Place your free hand on your upper stomach. Focus on keeping your core tight and bringing the dumbbell over your working pec.

- *Hammer Strength rows* –x10–x10–x10

Core Work

- *Physio-Ball Weighted Crunch (10-lb. plate behind head)* –x10–x10–x10 Align the center of the physio-ball with the middle of your back. Now with a 10 lb. plate behind your head perform a crunch. Be sure to go all the way down and form your body to the ball during each rep.

- *Leg Lifts On Decline Bench* –x15–x15–x15 Using the decline bench, lie on your back with your feet towards the ground. Now hold on via the leg handles above your head and lift your knees to your chest. Be sure to lift your hips off the bench on each rep.

Power Plate Cool Down Protocol

- *30 sec. Quarter Squat (35 Light)*

- *30 sec. Quarter Squat (35 Heavy) (invert and evert ankles)*

- *30 sec. Toe Touch (35 Light)*

- *30 Sec. Full Squats (35 Heavy)*

- *30 sec. Hamstring Massage (40 Heavy)*. Sit down on the Power Plate with your legs straddling the center console. Now shift your hips back so that each hamstring is on the center of the Plate. For a greater massage have a partner push down on your thighs during the massage.

- *30 sec. Calves Massage (40 Heavy)*. Similar to the hamstring massage, but place your calves instead of your hamstrings on the center of the Plate. As in the hamstring massage, for a greater massage have a partner push down on your shins during the massage.

Skill Work

- *Mikan Drill* –x20–x20. **Scoring on both sides with ball outside the body**

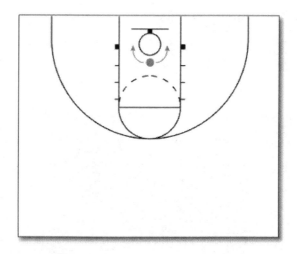

- *Hook Shot Drill With Movement In Paint* **(shuffle, carioca, backpedal, sprint)** –x10–x10–x10–x10

TUESDAY

Shooting Training

- *Swing Shooting* (5 from each side with 2 free throws between each set. Must hit 1 of 2 free-throws) –x10–x10–x10
- *Free-Throws* (keep track of makes out of 30) –x30
- *Vertical Jump Training*
- *Backboard Smacks*
  - (no step) –x4–x4
  - (1 step) –x4–x4
  - (3 steps) –x4–x4

Resistance Training

- *Overhead squats*–x8–x8. Start with your feet shoulder-hip width apart with the barbell above and slightly behind your head. Lock your elbows and keep them locked throughout the exercise. Now complete a parallel squat (thighs parallel to the ground) focusing on shifting your hips back. Push through your heels and sit back. Do not let your heels come off the floor or allow your knees to move forward over your toes. Keep your back tight and squeeze your abs. Maintain an upright 45-degree torso angle throughout the duration of the exercise.

- *Barbell Squats* –x8–x8–x6

- *Box Step-Ups* –x6–x6–x6. With a barbell on your back as if you were performing a squat, start with one foot on top of a box (20-24 in.) and the down foot up against the box on the floor. Push through the box with your heel and do not let your heel come off the box. Do not push off with your down foot. As you perform the step-up, maintain a tight back and squeeze your abs. Maintain a 45-degree torso angle. As your body rises on the box, lift your down leg through and finish with your thigh parallel to the ground with both your knee and toe up.

- *RDL's* –x6–x6–x6. Start holding a barbell against your thighs with your feet shoulder-hip width apart and knees slightly bent. Now, without bending your knees, shift your hips back and bring the barbell down to a point just past your knees. Bring the barbell slowly back up to the starting position. Maintain a tight back and abdomen, squeeze the shoulder blades together and lock the elbows throughout the duration of the exercise.

- *Physio-Ball Dumbbell Shoulder Press* –x10–x10–x10. Sit on a physio-ball and perform a shoulder press. Focus on squeezing your core region and keeping your back tight. Do not allow your elbows to go beyond 90-degrees.

- *Plate Raises (superset with dumbbell side raises)* –x10–x10. Hold a plate with one hand at 3 o'clock and the other at 9 o'clock. Lock your elbows and do not bend your arms during the exercise. Begin with the plate slightly below your waist, against your thighs. Now raise the plate in front of your body until you can look through the barbell hole. Control the plate as you lower it to the starting position.

- *Dumbbell Side Raises (superset with plate raises)* –x10–x10

Core Work

- *Reverse Hypers On Box* –x10–x10–x10. Using a box that approximately is waist high, hold the far end of the box with each hand. Keep your hands shoulder width apart. Now lift your legs off the ground towards the ceiling. Lock your knees, keeping your legs straight at all times. Maintain a tight back.

- *Physio-ball low back extension* –x10–x10–x10. Using a physio-ball, lie down on your stomach, ensuring that the center of the ball is at the center of your abdomen. Place your feet shoulder-hip width apart and hands behind your head. Now extend your back to the point where your body is parallel to the ground. Do not extend past this point. Remember to form your body to the ball on the way down in each rep.

Court Work

- *Warm-Up And Stretch*

- *Active Warm-Up With the Ball*

- *Speed Ladder With Dribble (each repetition equals one run of the entire ladder)*

- *Forward 1 foot in each ladder hole* –x2

- *Forward 2 feet in each ladder hole* –x2

- *Lateral 2 feet in each ladder hole* –x2

- *Lateral 1 foot in and 1 foot out in each ladder hole* –x2. Start with right foot in ladder hole and left foot outside of ladder hole. Alternate in and out as you laterally move down the ladder making sure that both the right and left foot hit inside each ladder hole.

- *Forward Ickey Shuffle* –x2. Start with left foot in ladder hole. Step with right foot into ladder hole. Step outside the next ladder hole with left foot. Step in the ladder hole where left foot is outside with right foot. Step inside ladder hole with left foot. Step outside next ladder hole with right foot. Repeat pattern for entire ladder.

- *Backward Ickey Shuffle*–x2. Start with right foot in ladder hole. Step with left foot into ladder hole. Step outside the next ladder hole with right foot. Step in the ladder hole where right is outside with left foot. Step inside ladder hole with right foot. Step outside next ladder hole with left foot. Repeat pattern for entire ladder.

- *Power Band Drill (3 bands)* –x10. Start with the bands attached around your waist and stand directly in front of the rim at a distance of approximately three feet. Explode up towards the rim and score the ball ten times as quickly as possible either by dunking or performing a lay-up. It is important to have your training partner or coach move in all directions to provide resistance from all angles to challenge your leg strength and vertical explosion.

- *Horizontal and Vertical Band Attack (reps from both angles and last set without bands)* –x5–x5–x5. Start with the bands attached around your waist and stand near the baseline at a 45-degree angle from the rim at a distance of approximately four feet. With only one dribble and two steps explode up towards the rim and score. Perform the drill from the right and left sides of the rim. It is important to have the bands provide resistance at all times, meaning have the bands taut throughout the drill.

- *Band shooting and agility from elbow and baseline with shuf-fle/carioca combo (last set without bands)* –x5–x5–x5. Start with the bands attached to your waist and stand on the baseline. Shuffle out to the elbow of the foul line against band resistance. Plant at the elbow and carioca back towards the baseline. When you reach the baseline, turn and sprint to the elbow. Have a teammate pass you the ball when you reach the foul line and score. It is important that the bands offer zero resistance during your shot, so have your training partner or coach follow you as you sprint to the elbow to receive the ball.

THURSDAY

Resistance Training

- *Barbell shrugs* –x15–x15–x10

- *Straight bar curls (drop sets)* –x10+10+10,–x10+10+10. To perform a drop set, complete three consecutive sets of 10 with varying weights. For example, start with the barbell and two 5 lb. weights on each side. Complete the first set at this weight and take off one 5 lb. weight from each side for the second set. Immediately complete the second set and take off the final 5 lb. weight from each side. Then immediately complete the final set with just the barbell.

- *Close grip bench press (drop sets)* –x10+10+10,–x10+10+10. Grip the bar with a width that allows your hands to be inside of your shoulders to isolate the triceps. Perform drop sets as described above, but use heavier weights.

Core Work

- *Straight leg crunches* –x25

- *Bent knee crunches* –x25

- *Suitcase crunches* –x25. Begin by lying down with the legs extended. Raise the legs off the ground approximately 2 inches. From this position, perform a crunch by bringing your knees towards your chest and your elbows towards your knees. Touch your elbows to your knees and return back to the starting position.

- *Toe pickers* –x25. Lie down on your back with your legs extended. Lift your legs to a 90-degree angle so that the soles of your feet are facing towards the ceiling. Extend your arms towards the ceiling also. Now while keeping your arms and legs extended, touch your toes.

- *Rockies* –x15. Lie down on your back with your legs extended. Lift your legs to a 90-degree angle so that your toes are pointing towards the ceiling. Now lift your hips off the ground by flexing your abs and pushing your toes toward the ceiling. Keep your legs extended at all times and do not allow your knees to move towards your head.

- *Grinders* –x25–x25. Lie down on your back with your legs extended. Lift both legs off the ground approximately 2 inches. Now pull one knee towards your head and touch your opposite elbow to that knee. Hold this position until your partner or coach says 1, at which point drive your opposite knee to your opposite elbow. Continue this pattern until you complete 25 reps only alternating positions on your training partner or coach's command.

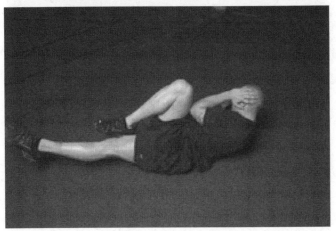

CHAPTER 3

LEBRON JAMES' FOOTBALL CAREER

While LeBron was getting his national fame from basketball, in his earlier years in high school he was also an asset on the football field. As a wide receiver for St. Vincent-St. Mary's, during his sophomore year he caught 42 receptions for 820 yards, 7 of which were touchdowns, and **he earned a place on the first all-state team**.

The coach, Jay Brophy, saw LeBron as a combination of football players Harold Carmichael and Randy Moss. He was naturally strong, coordinated, and gifted, although Brophy suspected he might not be able to play throughout high school. The first day of LeBron's freshman year when Brophy was an assistant, he saw LeBron, who was 6'4" at the time, jump up and catch a one-handed pass.

He missed the start of his junior season because of a summer basketball game. This was when it was becoming clear that he might have to face a decision of choosing one sport over the other. However, in his junior year, he helped the Fighting Irish football team reach the state semifinals. He caught 61 passes for 1,245 yards and 16 touchdowns. After breaking his left wrist in an AAU basketball game before his senior football season, **he made the decision not to play**.

When LeBron told Brophy, he understood and the two maintained a healthy relationship. Although, he never got rid of LeBron's equipment, and when he saw him in the locker room, would often tease him to come back for a few more games.

Alas, LeBron would stick with basketball. He concedes that if he couldn't enter the NBA draft, he likely would have geared his life towards the NFL. He says he misses football, however, he does not let his children play. He told ESPN *"Only basketball, baseball and soccer are allowed in my house... until they understand how physical and how demanding the game is. Then they can have their choice in high school."* Thus, despite his love for the game, his love for safety prevails.

CHAPTER 4

EARLY NBA - CAVALIERS

In the 2003 NBA draft, LeBron James was selected by the Cleveland Cavaliers, as the **first overall pick**. The 6'8" 240-pound teenager signed a three-year contract for just under $13 million.

His rookie season was impressive. In his debut against the Sacramento Kinds, LeBron put up 25 points. He would later set a record for being **the youngest player to score over 40 in a game**, when he put 41 points up against the New Jersey Nets.

The Cavaliers finished off the season with a 35-47 record, and were unable to make the playoffs. That said, LeBron added growth to the team. The record was an 18 game improvement from the previous year, and LeBron joined the ranks of Oscar Robertson and Michael Jordan, as being the only other player in the group to score over 20 points, get 5 rebounds, and have 5 assists, per game in their rookie year. These statistics won him the *Rookie of the Year award*.

James would continue setting records. In the 2004-2005 season he became **the youngest player in history to get a triple double**. That season he also was selected for his first All-Star Game. During the game, which was won by the Eastern Conference, he scored 13 points, got 8 rebounds, and made 6 assists. A few months later in March, LeBron scored 56 points in a game against the Toronto Raptors, which was a career-high and a record for the Cavaliers. At only 20 years old, he also became **the youngest player to make the All-NBA Team in history**. The Cavaliers finished their season with a 42-40 record, again not making the playoffs.

LeBron set two other "youngest person" records in 2006. The first one was at the All-Star game. After again leading his team to victory, this time scoring 29 points**, he was awarded the All-Star Game MVP**. The second came as a result of averaging over 30 points for the season; he scored an average of 31.4 points and got 7 rebounds per game. Additionally, and arguably most important, the Cavaliers made the playoffs for the first time since 1998. The Cavs went on to beat the Wizards in a five game series, with LeBron putting up a triple-double and a game winning shot in Game 1 and Game 3, respectively. They lost in the second round to the Pistons, but LeBron was finally getting a step closer to his dream of winning an NBA Championship.

After the playoffs, **LeBron resigned with the Cavs**. This time, he signed for a 3-year, $60 million contract. The following year the Cavs won 50 games. Though James was ridiculed for lazy play in the beginning of the season, he rounded out with averages of 27.3 points 6.7 rebounds, and 1.6 steals per game. Cleveland advanced to the Conference Finals as the second seed and James scored 29 of the Cavaliers last 30 points (including a game winning shot) to overtake the Pistons. He ended up scoring a total of 48 points, grabbing 9 rebounds, and dishing out 7 assists in the game. In 2012 ESPN put the performance in the number four spot on the best performances in playoff history. However, in the finals LeBron's averages of 22 points, 7 rebounds, and 6.8 assists per game, were not nearly enough. The San Antonio Spurs beat Cleveland in a mere 4 games.

The 2007-2008 looked good on paper for LeBron, but not so much the Cavaliers. **He won the All-Star Game MVP for the second time and became the Cavaliers' all-time leading scorer.** The previous record holder, Brad Daugherty, had to play over 100 more games than LeBron to do so. He averaged 30 points per game and capped of the season with seven triple-doubles. However, Cleveland ended the season with a 45-37 record and a fourth playoff seed. They beat the Wizards again in the first round, but lost to the Boston Celtics in a seven game series thereafter.

The following year LeBron began to make a name for himself defensively. In 2009, after racking up 93 total blocks (23 of which were chase-downs) he was voted **second in the Defensive Player of the Year** category. He also led Cleveland in points, rebounds, assists, steals and blocks. His dominance translated to the team, as well. The Cavs finished with a 66-16 record. If they had only one more, they would have had the best record in franchise history. That year, **LeBron won the league MVP Award**, becoming the first Cavalier ever to do so. He had averages of 28.4 points, 7.6 rebounds, 7.2 assists, 1.7 steals, and 1.2 blocks per game.

After sweeping the Pistons and the Atlanta Hawks in the first two rounds, the Cavaliers faced off with the Orlando Magic to earn the Conference Title. Despite coming out on fire, scoring 49 points by shooting 66% from the field, and hitting a game-winning shot in Game 2, the Magic overtook the Cavs in 6 games. For the series, LeBron's averages were 38.5 points, 8.3 rebounds, and 8 assists per game.

The following year (in 2010) LeBron adjusted to playing point guard in the wake of teammate injuries. In doing so, he averaged 29.7 points, 8.6 assists, 7.3 rebounds, 1.6 steals and 1 block per game. His performance resulted in a **second MVP Award**. Cleveland beat the Bulls in the first round but lost the Celtics in the second round. A poor playoff performance relative to previous years led to a high degree of criticism.

CHAPTER 5

THE DECISION AND BACKLASH

"I like criticism. It makes you strong."

- LeBron James

On July 1, 2010, at precisely 12:01am, **LeBron became a free agent**. Aside from Cleveland Cavaliers, rumors about his interest going to the Chicago Bulls, Los Angeles Clippers, Miami Heat, New York Knicks, and New Jersey Nets, permeated the media. On July 8, ESPN ran a live special dramatically titled *The Decision*, which ran for 75 minutes.

After waiting for about 30 minutes after the program began, James came out in a public statement, broadcasted from the Boys and Girls Club in Greenwich Connecticut, that **he would go to play with the Miami Heat**, joining Dwayne Wade and Chris Bosh. LeBron said verbatim:

"In this fall... this is very tough... in this fall I'm going to take my talents to South Beach and join the Miami Heat. I feel like it's going to give me the best opportunity to win and to win for multiple years, and not only just to win in the regular season or just to win five games in a row or three games in a row, I want to be able to win championships. And I feel like I can compete down there."

The reception was huge. Just under 10 million people tuned in to watch the show in the United States, and over 13 million people were watching at the time of the announcement. It was the most watched cable show of the evening and Cleveland topped all of the markets. However, the show, although few knew it at the time, was actually a fundraiser, and it raised $2.5 million for the Boys & Girls Club charity and an additional $3.5 million from advertisements for other charities.

Almost immediately, **intense criticism followed**. Cleveland fans and Cavalier players and leadership outwardly expressed their disapproval. Dan Gilbert, majority owner, wrote a public letter criticizing LeBron's decision and presentation. Even Michael Jordan and Magic Johnson criticized LeBron for making something of a cowardly decision. Despite all of the backlash, LeBron stuck with his decision and moved to Miami to join Bosh and Wade in the hopes of winning a championship.

CHAPTER 6

TRANSITION TO HEAT

LeBron was welcomed to Miami in spectacular fashion. The Heat threw a welcome party at the American Airlines Arena. This set the tone for the following season as everyone but Miami fans depicted LeBron as the stereotypical evil sports man. When Miami faced off against Cleveland that season he was booed every time he had possession of the ball. Despite this, he scored 38 points to win the game.

The Heat made it to the finals in LeBron's first season. However, the Dallas Mavericks would win the series in 6 games. People criticized LeBron's end-of-game play, as *his fourth quarter averages were only 3 points per game.*

Losing in the finals took a serious emotional toll on LeBron. **He made a firm commitment to work harder than he had ever worked before,** during the off-season. *He enlisted Hakeem Olajuwon to train him* as he specifically wanted to work on his low-post game.

Olajuwon would do a range of drills, often beginning by going up and down the court doing one dribble spin moves, which could then be replicated on the post. He then showed LeBron a number of quick post moves. LeBron starts with his back to the basket. He pivots to face the hoop, swings the ball from the outside of his body, takes a power dribble, and slams the ball. The key to all of these drills was the repetition.

The 2011-2012 season featured a new LeBron James. Although the season was a bit shorter due to the lockout, he still finished with 27.1 points, 7.9 rebounds, 6.2 assists, and 1.9 steals, per game, **earning his third MVP award**.

When the playoffs came around the Heat knew anything less than winning would be a disappointment. LeBron had an incredible performance where he scored 40 points, had 18 rebounds, and dished out 9 assists to beat the Pacers in Indiana in Game 4.

The Heat moved onto the Conference Finals against the Boston Celtics. Boston was able to gain a 3-2 lead in the series. However, in Game 6 LeBron scored 45 points shooting 73% from the field. The Heat won both Game 6 and 7 to advance to the finals against the Oklahoma City Thunder.

The Heat won the series in 5 games. In the last game LeBron put up a triple double and was rewarded with **his first championship trophy** and the honor of the **Finals MVP**. He averaged 28.6 points, 10.2 rebounds, and 7.4 assists per game, in the series.

The 2012-2013 only saw more improvements. The Heat were on fire, which was an apt description for the team. They went on the second longest winning streak in NBA history, winning 27 games in a row. Around this time in the winter LeBron was averaging 29.7 points and 7.8 assists per game. He was **voted MVP for the fourth time**, and received votes from all voters except for one person. The Heat finished the season with 66 wins and 16 losses.

They made it to the finals with relative ease. This time, they would be facing the San Antonio Spurs. After having a rough start in the series and falling behind 2-3, LeBron scored another triple-double in Game 6. In the final game **LeBron scored 37 points to secure the win, again earning the title of MVP**.

As the 2013-2014 season came, many wondered what LeBron was capable of doing. In a game against the Charlotte Bobcats, **he scored a career-high 61 points**. His season averages ended up being 27.1 points, 6.9 rebounds, and 6.4 assists per game. He was also shooting 56.7% from the field.

Again, the **Heat progressed to the NBA Finals**, only the fourth team in NBA history to do so four years in a row. They faced the Spurs for the second time, **but this time would not take hold of the series**. Despite LeBron's series averages of 28 points, 7.8 rebounds, and 2 steals per game, San Antonio won the championship in five games.

CHAPTER 7

COMING HOME TO CLEVELAND

On July 11 2014, *Sports Illustrated* published an essay allegedly written by LeBron James entitled *"I'm Coming Home."* The essay was essentially the polar opposite as the TV special *The Decision*. These were his concluding remarks:

"I feel my calling here goes above basketball. I have a responsibility to lead, in more ways than one, and I take that very seriously. My presence can make a difference in Miami, but I think it can mean more where I'm from. I want kids in Northeast Ohio, like the hundreds of Akron third-graders I sponsor through my foundation, to realize that there's no better place to grow up. Maybe some of them will come home after college and start a family or open a business. That would make me smile. Our community, which has struggled so much, needs all the talent it can get.

In Northeast Ohio, nothing is given. Everything is earned. You work for what you have.

I'm ready to accept the challenge. I'm coming home."

The following day **LeBron signed a two-year contract with Cleveland** for $42.1 million. Shortly after, the Cavs signed Kevin Love and Kyrie Irving to add to LeBron's supporting cast.

Despite the backlash and borderline hatred that permeated Ohio, and of course, Cleveland, when LeBron initially left, they essentially welcomed him home with open arms. Of course, his character change played a role in this, and his commitment to staying in Cleveland certainly seemed more genuine. But despite some of the previous frustration, fans, as well as the city were simply happy to see him back on the court again and fighting to win for the city.

The 2014-2015 season did not get off to the smoothest start. LeBron sat out for the longest period of time of his career due to an injury. However, he bounced back after two weeks being sidelined in the winter, and he bounced back strong. After finishing the regular season with per game averages of 25.3 points, 6 rebounds and 7.4 assists, he earned the title of **Cleveland's all-time assists leader.**

After beating the Chicago Bulls in the second round of the playoffs Cleveland advanced to play the Atlanta Hawks in the conference finals. Unfortunately, when Cleveland advanced to the finals to play Stephen Curry and the Golden State Warriors, key member Kyrie Irving fell to an injury, as had Kevin Love had a bit earlier. Despite averaging 35.8 points, 13.3 rebounds and 8.8 assists per game, the Warriors won comfortable. However, contrary to previous championship performances that many criticized, the media looked upon his play positively.

The summer following the championships, LeBron opted out of his contract. However, he was not leaving Cleveland again. **He has signed a two-year contract.**

On November 2, 2015, **LeBron reached the milestone of scoring 25,000 points, and became the youngest player in NBA history to do so.**

CHAPTER 8

OLYMPIC
TRANSFORMATION

LeBron's experiences and public perceptions throughout his three Olympic experiences in many ways serve as a microcosm for his development as an athlete overall.

His first experience came at the 2004 Olympics in Athens, Greece. He averaged a mere 14.6 minutes per game, and the United States came in a disappointing third place. Since adding professional NBA players to the lineup, this was the first time the United States did not return home with a gold medal. James' averages, just 5.8 points and 2.6 rebounds per game, were low in correspondence with his time spent on the court. He openly spoke against the team leadership, criticizing them not giving him a fair chance to make a difference. ***He was criticized publicly as ungrateful and disrespectful.***

In 2006, James competed internationally for the United States in Japan at the 2006 FIBA World Championship. Though his stats were more impressive, putting up averages of 13.9 points, 4.8 rebounds, and 4.1 assists per game, the USA finished with a bronze yet again. Further, his attitude saw little improvement. Bruce Bowen, a teammate and long term NBA basketball player, was public about LeBron's negative attitude towards staff members and teammates.

Thus, when the 2008 Olympics rolled around, before being put on the roster James was spoken to by senior staff members informing him that ***he needed to change his attitude if he wanted to play***. He was allowed to participate in the qualifying series, the FIBA Americas Championship 2007. Against Argentina, he scored 31 points, and throughout the series averaged 18.1 points, 3.6 rebounds, and 4.7 assists. Team USA won all ten games, received the gold medal, and qualified for the next Olympics.

In 2008 in Beijing, China, a lot of controversy arose over comments Dwayne Wade made about being compensated. James publicly stated, *"I don't think we understood what it meant to put on a USA uniform and all the people that we were representing in 2004. We definitely know that now."* His words translated well in the games, as the United States went undefeated and reclaimed their spot on the top of the podium.

LeBron did not again compete internationally until the 2012 Olympics in London, however, he completely took charge of the team. He became **the first player to put up a triple-double in Olympic basketball history,** as he scored 11 points, got 14 rebounds, and made 12 assists against Argentina. The USA again faced Spain in the Olympic finals. LeBron scored 19 points leading the USA to another gold medal. That year, he won the **NBA MVP Award,** an **NBA championship,** and **NBA Finals MVP,** and an **Olympic gold medal.** And further, his public image regarding the international sporting event was restored.

CHAPTER 9

KING JAMES' WORKOUTS AND TRAINING REGIMEN

LeBron is frequently cited as a rare and unbelievable physical specimen. There is no doubt that there is some level of natural physical ability that LeBron possesses, but his physicality does not come from thin air. **LeBron works incredibly hard**, and has not just dedicated his life to training on the court. Basketball is a lifestyle; he monitors what he eats, how much he sleeps, and does tons of off-court exercises to stay healthy and be **able to outrun, outmuscle, and outdo his opponents in every capacity**.

Diet

In the summer of 2014 LeBron decided to go on a very strict diet. Weighing about 270 pounds prior, he lost around 20 pounds by only eating meat, fish, vegetables, and fruits. ***The low carb ketogenic-style Paleo diet*** was inspired by Ray Allen, who followed the same regimen, and not only lost weight, but reported being fitter, lighter, and just feeling better. One example of a meal was an arugula salad with chicken, strawberries, mangoes and cashews topped with olive oil/lemon vinaigrette dressing. After following this strict regimen for 67 days, LeBron lost a bit too much weight, and has since put some back on. However, it made him more conscious about food. Someone who used to not pay attention to what he put in his body became very aware.

Here is a sample day of what LeBron eats:

Meal 1: Two 8 ounce glasses of water, 10 grams of L-glutamine mixed with water

Meal 2: 1 whole wheat bagel, 1 tbsp. peanut butter, half cup cottage cheese, half cup strawberries, 1 multivitamin and mineral tablet

Meal 3: 1 scoop protein powder (2oz) - 22 grams protein, 1 cup orange juice, 1 medium banana, 1.5 cup 1% milk

Meal 4: (lean roast beef sub): 6" whole wheat bun, 4 ounces lean roast beef, 1 cup lettuce, 1 tomato cut into slices, 1/2 oz. low fat cheddar cheese, 2 tbsp. mustard, 1 cup 1% milk

Meal 5: 1 granola bar -Quaker, 1/2 cup blueberries, 1 tbsp. brown sugar, 1 cup low fat natural yogurt, 1 apple, half glass of low fat milk

Meal 6: 1 cup strawberries, 1 cup low fat strawberry yogurt, 1 scoop (2oz) vanilla protein powder - 22 grams protein, 1/2 tbsp. honey, 1 cup 1% milk, 1 cup orange juice, 5 grams creatine monohydrate

Meal 7 (chicken teriyaki): 3 oz. boneless chicken breasts, 1/3 cup prepared teriyaki sauce, 1/3 cup orange juice, 1 tsp cornstarch, 1/3 tsp ginger, 1/2 tbsp. extra virgin olive oil, 1.5 cup small broccoli florets, half can (4 ounces) sliced water chestnuts, half cup rice, 1 cup pure water

This might seem like a lot of food to most people, however, LeBron's days are jam packed with exercise. Thus, it's important that he fuels his body properly and constantly.

Gym Regimen

LeBron has said that he begins every day by icing his back and his feet, followed by 30 minutes of stretching and yoga before either going to the gym or going to do court work.

Here are some of his **regular off-court training routines:**

Monday - LeBron James Workout				
#	Exercise	Sets	Reps	Notes
Superset 1	Pushups	3	until failure	Focus on keeping the right pushup form for the best results
	Pull Ups		10	Rest 45 seconds
Superset 2	Dumbbell Snatch	3	5	Reps for each Arm
	Single-Arm Cable Row		10	
General Notes: 45 second rest between supersets				

Dumbbell Snatch

Tuesday - LeBron James Workout				
#	Exercise	Sets	Reps	Notes
Superset 1	Dumbbell Squat	3	8 to 14	
	Swiss-Ball Hip Raise and Leg Curl		10 to 12	
Superset 2	Dumbbell Step Up	3	10	Do with one leg then switch to next
	Single-Leg Standing Dumbbell Calf Raise		12	Do with each leg
General Notes: 45 Seconds rest between supersets.				

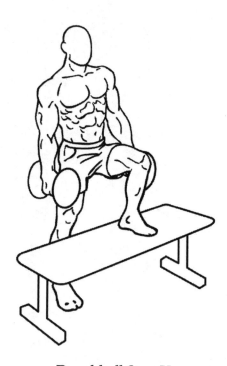

Dumbbell Step Up

Thursday - LeBron James Workout				
#	Exercise	Sets	Reps	Notes
Superset 1	Dumbbell Incline Bench press	3	10	
	Lat Pull-down		10	
Superset 2	Single-Arm Dumbbell Shoulder Press	3	6 to 10	Do with each leg
	Single Arm Neutral Grip Dumbbell Row		10	Switch to other direction

General Notes: 45 Seconds rest between supersets.

Dumbbell Shoulder Press

Friday - LeBron James Workout				
#	Exercise	Sets	Reps	Notes
Superset 1	Single-leg Squat	3	3 to 6	Do with one leg then switch to next
	Single-Leg Swiss Ball Leg Curl		10	Aim to do with each leg
Superset 2	Dumbbell Side Lunge	3	10	Do with one leg then switch to next
	Unstable Jump Rope		45 sec	Skip on an absorbent surface such as a stretching match. Doing this increases your knee workout.

General Notes: 45 Seconds rest between supersets.

Single Leg Swiss Ball Leg Curl

LeBron does take **off-days**, which to the average person, are far from "off." Although his off day varies based on scheduling, it is jam-packed with rehab and looks like this:

30 minutes on stationary bike

Breakfast

Rehydration

Cavaliers Practice

Cold tub

Massage

Stretching

Muscle stimulation

3-hour nap

Stretching with specialized equipment

Massage

Cryotherapy

Dinner

Conditioning

LeBron has averaged anywhere from 36 minutes to over 42 minutes per game, since joining the NBA. Thus, his conditioning is incredibly important in measuring how successful he'll be at any given point, and especially in the 4th quarter. He was once quoted in an interview, *"To improve stamina, the treadmill is good, but the exercise bike is tougher and works more of your body. Do a 10-mile ride uphill, and you know you've had a workout."*

However, LeBron has a lot of other drills in his repertoire that aid in his conditioning.

In one drill he goes back and forth on the court, receiving leading passes. He receives the pass, lays it in for a dunk and immediately turns around to complete the shot at the opposite end. He does this at full speed, for 2-3 minutes.

Basketball Drills

Of course LeBron does a lot of basketball drills to hone his skills. Included in these, which are the keys to many player successes, are repetitive drills. After doing some jump roping and squats to warm up, LeBron will begin a shooting series.

Often he'll go out to the right wing and make, not take, **10 spot-up jump shots**.

While mixing in some strength and conditioning in between, he'll go to the top of the key to make another 10 spot up jump shots. Finally, he'll go to the left side to do the same. He'll then do the same from the corners, and when his legs are good and tired, will go to make five free throws.

The next basketball drill LeBron will do is a **one-dribble pull-up jump shot**, starting from the right side. After receiving a pass he'll take a quick dribble to the same side and take a quick release shot. He makes four of these before moving on. From here, he moves directly to the top of the key, and does the same drill, but this time with two dribbles. He doesn't have a set routine, sometimes he'll crossover, other times he'll go between the legs, etc. Again, he makes four.

2-DRIBBLE PULL-UP JUMP SHOT
TOP OF THE KEY – RIGHT/LEFT x 4 MAKES

He then makes four shots from two dribble pull-ups from the left side. LeBron concludes this series with another 5 made free throws, before taking a quick breather.

The next drill consists of **running hook shots**. Starting on one side he'll catch the ball with his back to the basket. Then, before faking the opposite way, he'll take on dribble and go towards the basket for a hook shot. He'll make five of these before immediately transitioning to fade away shots from the same side. Again, catching the ball with his back to the basket he'll take one dribble, but instead of going towards the hoop, will pivot, fade-away and take a shot. After he makes five, he'll stay on the same side, and do fade-aways pivoting the opposite way, to practice with the opposite shoulder.

After repeating the sequence on the opposite side of the court LeBron immediately begins practicing an **up and under post up move**. Catching the ball with his back to the basket, he takes one dribble and pivots to face the hoop. As he pivots he fakes a shot, then goes under the fake for a short range shot.

Again, he makes 5 more free throws.

Depending on the day, LeBron will then choose a number, usually between 5 and 7, which will be the number of **3-point spot up shots** he makes from 5 different spots on the court – the corners, the wings, and the top of the key. This is followed by 15 free throw makes.

Another drill LeBron often does is the **"Down Screen and Pop"**. He goes down to set a screen at the block, and then pops out to the corner 3-point line. From there, he'll do one of three moves. He'll either catch and shoot quickly, fake a shot and drive to the basket, or jab, take a dribble, and then pull up for a jump shot.

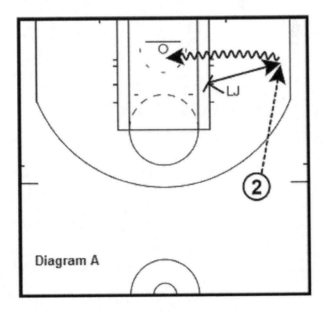

Diagram A

Another offensive drill he does is when he gets the ball at the top of the key. He'll hold the ball quickly in triple threat, and use a series of fakes before finding an avenue to take a one dribble step-back shot.

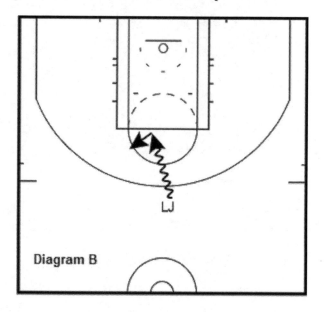

Diagram B

CHAPTER 10
PHILANTHROPY AND PERSONAL LIFE

Philanthropy

Various estimates to LeBron James' current net worth are anywhere from $270 million to $375 million. He has already made over $150 million just in NBA salaries and has numerous huge endorsements including Augemars Piguet, Coca-Cola, Dunkin' Brands, McDonald's, State Farm, Samsung, and of course, Nike. When LeBron entered the NBA, Nike, Adidas, and Reebok were offering him different sums of money for endorsements. Ultimately, Nike won out offering him $90 million. It is estimated that LeBron makes a salary of around $46 million dollars per year through his endorsements as well as his NBA contract. He's one of the best paid NBA players and one of the best paid athletes.

Nike has done well by LeBron. In 2012 they generated $300 million in retail sales in the United States for his signature shoes. While he hasn't overcome Michael Jordan in terms of becoming the largest shoe empire, his brand, the LeBron X's do quite well, and in 2013 he led all the NBA players in shoe sales.

Fenway Sports Group became the global marketer of his rights in 2011. In this deal, LeBron was given stakes with the football club Liverpool F.C. He also had a stake in Beats Electronics long before they became popular, and received an estimated $30 million from Apple's acquisition. Because of this, LeBron acts in numerous commercials, becoming an athlete also known for his acting skills.

While LeBron certainly does live a life of luxury (he sold his house in Miami for over $13 million and bought a new house in Akron for $9.2 million) he still does a fair amount of philanthropy.

LeBron's mansion in Miami

Notably, in 2005 LeBron established his own charity – the *LeBron James Family Foundation* –, which is based in his hometown of Akron. The organization holds a yearly bike-a-thon in Akron to raise money for different causes. He also uses the funds to donate equipment and facilities to his high school Alma Mater, St. Vincent-St. Mary. In addition to other initiatives, in 2021 the foundation will be able to provide up to 2,300 for scholarships to the University of Akron.

In addition to his own charity he is a big supporter of the Boys & Girls

Club of America, Children's Defense Fund, and ONEXONE.

Activism

LeBron has also become a more and more political figured over the years. He has been ranked by *Forbes* to be one of the world's most influential athletes, and he has used his status to speak about issues, primarily racism. Beginning in 2008, LeBron donated $20,000 to a committee to help elect Barack Obama.

When Trayvon Martin was shot and killed in 2012, LeBron and his Heat teammates took a photograph in hooded sweatshirts while bowing their heads to make a statement, and posted it on twitter. When Los Angeles Clippers owner Donald Sterling made outwardly racist comments, James came out and bluntly said, "There is no room for Donald Sterling in our league." When another young black man, Mike Brown, was killed in Ferguson, Missouri, James posted an illustration on Instagram and Twitter of Trayvon Martin and Mike Brown walking toward a heavenly light.

Thus, LeBron has used his influence to talk about political and societal issues he deems important.

kingjames · 12 months ago   + Follow

As a society how do we do better and stop things like this happening time after time!! I'm so sorry to these families. Violence is not the answer people. Retaliation isn't the solution as well. #PrayersUpToTheFamilies #WeHaveToDoBetter

300.2k likes   19.2k comments   Instagram

Personal Life

LeBron married Savannah Brinson, his high school sweetheart, on September 14, 2013. They have three children since then. First they had two sons—LeBron James, Jr., who was born on October 6, 2004, and Bryce Maximus James, born on June 14, 2007. And they have one daughter, Zhuri James.

LeBron grew up without a father in Akron, Ohio. He has spoken openly about how this affected him and how it helped him become the man he is today. Despite the difficulties that this caused for LeBron, it has made him quite a family man. He places a lot of value and emphasis on family, and makes sure to spend quality time with his wife and kids despite his busy workout schedule. He often watches *Tom and Jerry* with his kids.

He loves listening to hip hop, notably Jay-Z, Kanye West, and Drake. His favorite movies include *Gladiator* and *Friday*. He also enjoys reading; some of his favorite books are *The Hunger Games*, *The Tipping Point*, and *Decoded*. And finally, he enjoys watching sports of all kinds and playing the video game NBA 2K14 in his free time.

Here's what LeBron says about his need for the music: *"I need music. It's like my heartbeat, so to speak. It keeps me going no matter what's going on – bad games, press, whatever!"*.

CHAPTER 11

LEBRON'S SUPERSITIONS

The Chalk Toss

Unlike many prominent athletes, LeBron does not have any superstitions that he follows religiously or nervously makes sure to do before every game. However, his pre-game chalk toss is a habit he has become renowned for.

After sprinkling chalk on each of his hands, the crowd plays close attention and prepares. As he throws it up into the air, the entire crowd too throws up their hands in the air.

Afterwards he claps his hands a few times to get the rest of the chalk out, then puts one fist to his mouth, followed by the other. He says he started it as a way to simply get focused before a game. He enjoyed how the crowd took to enjoying it at home, but even when he is away, he still does it at the games. He often gets booed by the opposing fans, which he says he enjoys it and it motivates him to perform well.

The Headband

Until very recently, the headband was part of LeBron's image. He was rarely seen not wearing one on the court. However, a superstition arose from an instance where the headband fell off, and now he is usually seen without it. In the 2013 NBA finals against the Spurs, during Game 6, his headband was knocked off. That game, he played an amazing second half, recording a triple-double, and taking over the game.

The following game, Game 7, he played with a headband, and lost the championship. In March 2015, LeBron started his first-ever headband-less game, and now does not wear them. He claims it was to look like his team-mates and enhance unity, but of course no one can be sure.

Why Does LeBron Wear #23?

In LeBron's childhood rooms he had a wall of posters dedicated to Michael Jordan. Jordan was his idol, and so in high school, he wore the number 23, to *"pay homage to MJ,"* LeBron has said. When he came to the NBA, he still sported 23, which was somewhat controversial as it is a number so frequently associated with Jordan.

When LeBron went to Miami, he switched to the number 6. At that time, he made a public statement that no one should wear number 23. He said:

"I just think what Michael Jordan has done for the game has to be recognized some way soon. There would be no LeBron James, no Kobe Bryant, no Dwayne Wade if there wasn't Michael Jordan first."

However, when he returned to Cleveland, he also returned to the number 23, feeling that he was more deserving having won two NBA titles. He declared, *"I felt like the time was right to go back to it. I am a champion, and I have earned the right to wear it."*

Michael Jordan has publicly stated that he sees no problem with LeBron wearing his number, as he "does not own it." It remains, and most likely will remain, a topic of conversation throughout LeBron's career.

CHAPTER 12

BASKETBALL PHILOSOPHY

*"Ask me to steal, block out, sacrifice, lead, dominate. ANYTHING.
But it's not what you ask of me, it's what I ask of MYSELF."*

- LeBron James

Injury Prevention

Nothing has stressed and irritated LeBron more than not being able to play. He does everything in his power to make sure he approaches the court healthy. Having mainly issues in his lower back, to combat this, he does a lot of Yoga, stretching and Pilates. He also ices his back first thing in the morning. Although he has the benefit of access to very high quality and expensive technology, incorporating the amount of time of recovery into his schedule is central to his success.

Versatility

LeBron's training philosophy has centered on making him the most well rounded player he can possibly be. This means identifying his weaknesses and isolating specific drills and parts of the game to focus and hone in on different skills. He can handle the ball, he can shoot from the outside, he can post up, and he can certainly drive. He's also a great defender. These are all things that he has spent countless hours focusing on so he can execute from all points on the floor during the game.

Changing the Court Focus

With LeBron's versatile basketball skills and abilities, his strategies in games are to change the focus of his strengths. When he drives successfully, and the defense begins to collapse on him, he will start shooting from the outside, or drive and kick the ball out. Conversely, if he is shooting well from beyond the arc, he'll fake shots and go and drive. His game strategy is to never let the defense get fully settled, and constantly change up his tactics. This prevents them from being able to effectively double-team him, and opens up more opportunities for his teammates.

Belief

LeBron James hardly remembers a time in his life when he was not under the spotlight. Thus, dealing with pressure has been central to both his mental and physical preparation, and has designed much of his philosophy when it comes to the game of basketball.

Central to his personal philosophy is belief. He has said in an interview:

"There has always been a lot of pressure on me, so nerves are something I quickly conquered. Every time I step on the court I believe I am going to be on the winning team. Of course, it doesn't always work out that way, but you have to have the belief."

Thus, not just saying to oneself that he'll win, but truly believing it, is central to LeBron's philosophy. Feeling confident, believing in his own abilities as well as those of his teammates are central to victory.

Distraction

He always shies away from obsession. Although most average people would consider LeBron obsessed with the amount of work he puts into basketball, he believes in clearing his mind from time to time, in order to maximize performance. To do this, he reads many books. He has said:

"It just slows my mind down. It gives me another outlet. Throughout the playoffs, all you think about is basketball. All you want to do is play basketball. But at the same time it can become a lot. It can come to a point where it's overloading to the mind and you think about it too much. It's hard to get away from it because you're playing every other day, you talk about it every single day, you prepare every single day. The reading has given me an opportunity before the game, it just gives me an opportunity to read and think about something else. It's made me comfortable."

Apparently, he is a very big fan of *The Hunger Games* among other series.

Team Work

Many have criticized LeBron in the past for not scoring enough, or not putting up enough shots, especially in the off season. However, this is not for lack of care. LeBron, especially over the course of his NBA career, has become an incredibly passer. And, he knows that he cannot win alone. He shares the ball because he knows just because he scores the most points, his team will not necessarily win. He believes that unity, and cohesiveness are integral to success.

No Shortcuts

Finally, while LeBron is well aware, as is everyone, that he naturally has certain physical capacities that are unobtainable to many others, this hardly prevents him from becoming the best player he can be. He puts effort into every exercise – on the court and off the court. He realizes that the often-cited "little things" – stretching, diet, gym exercises, etc. – are what makes the difference between good and great players. Thus, he will always be the first person to get to the gym, the last person to leave, and the first person to begin off-season workouts.

CHAPTER 13

TOP 5 MOTIVATIONAL LESSONS FROM LEBRON JAMES

Dream as if you'll live forever, live as if you'll die today.

- Lebron James

1. Extrinsic and Intrinsic

When it comes to motivational lessons to be learned from LeBron, it can be broken down with the fusion of two different motivational forces – *intrinsic* and *extrinsic*.

In terms of extrinsic motivation, LeBron has an excellent source. He believes that thriving off of extrinsic forces can be immensely valuable. There is no player that is scrutinized by fans and the media as intensely as LeBron. And while the superstar doesn't believe that letting it get to his head is productive, he does believe that using that as motivation to fuel his will to win is certainly a good thing.

LeBron still has a lot to prove, especially to the city of Cleveland. He came back with the promise of doing everything in his ability to win championships for the city, and he has set up that external motivation to fuel his drive every day.

Further, he often cites his family as a source of motivation. Wanting to make his friends and family proud is a source of motivation that he prides himself on, to make the sport larger than a simple physical act.

He also believes intrinsic motivation is vital.

If LeBron retired today, he would still be considered one of the greatest players of all time. But intrinsically, he is motivated by the fact that he can do more, be better, and become even greater.

His motivation to become the best player he can be, leave all of his effort on the court, and continue working on his game until it is perfected, is an important lesson for not just athletes to learn, but people in all realms of life. Satisfaction, to LeBron, is never fully felt. It is only dreamt about.

2. Facing Fears

LeBron has commended Michael Jordan for not having a fear of failure. LeBron struggles with this more than one might think. He *does* fear failure, like most people, but also recognizes he must put the fear of failure behind him at times. Whatever fears athletes may have, LeBron believes, should be used to motivate, not to inhibit.

3. Teammates

Much of LeBron's source of motivation, and what he believes should be a source of motivation for all athletes, is not to let his teammates down. Thus, depending on the game situation, etc., the meaning of not letting one's teammates down varies. Sometimes that means he needs to score 40 points, sometimes it means he needs to score 20. But doing everything in his power to get his team to win, is at the forefront of his concern.

4. Play Every Game Like It's Your Last

For every practice, game, drill, that LeBron does, he gets it into his mindset that it might be the last play he is doing. Adapting this mindset, he believes has helped him become the player he is today. He does not take being able to play the game for a living for granted, and cherishes every moment. This does more than increase his appreciation – it also enhances his game, focus, and drive.

5. Have Short-Term and Long-Term Goals

LeBron has cited the importance of having both short and long term goals. Short-term goals are important to keep track of progress, and motivate yourself on a smaller scale. However, long-term goals keep you motivated and keep your drive high.

CHAPTER 14

11 INTERESTING FACTS YOU DIDN'T KNOW ABOUT LEBRON

1. LeBron is ambidextrous. He does certain activities like writing and eating with his left hand, while on the other hand he shoots and makes layups using his right hand.

2. LeBron James was the first black man, and third man ever, to be featured in the cover page of the Vogue. It was very controversial because it mirrored a WWI *Destroy This Mad Brute* poster.

3. LeBron loves cereal. Some of his favorites are Fruity Pebbles, Frosted Flakes and Cinnamon Toast Crunch.

4. According to one estimate, when LeBron left Cleveland the first time he cost the city $24 million.

5. LeBron does not root for Ohio teams, and did not while growing up. He often sports a New York Yankees hat, which has been a topic of much controversy for Ohio fans.

6. One of the many places that James and his mother, Gloria, lived when he was growing up was 439 Hickory St. in Akron, Ohio. There is actual footage in a recent Beats by Dre headphones commercial that shows that house being torn down.

7. LeBron's second son, Bryce Maximus, was born on June 14th. This was during his trip to the finals during 2007, and has supposedly been a marker in LeBron's career to appreciate his own success.

8. LeBron said in a 2009 interview that the Los Angeles Lakers was his favorite team to play against.

9. Growing up LeBron had posters of all the NBA greats on his wall. Even before he got his own *Sports Illustrated* cover photograph, he made up a fake one with the saying, "Is he the next Michael Jordan" on it.

10. If LeBron did go to play in college, he has said the two main schools on his mind were Ohio State and University of North Carolina.

11. There is an interesting phenomenon called "The LeBron Effect" which is called so because of the "get-in" ticket prices for Cavaliers games spikes 108 percent to 245 percent when LeBron plays the game. That's especially true after Cavaliers winning streak.

CHAPTER 15

AWARDS AND HONORS

2015-2016 Season

- NBA Champion
- NBA Finals MVP
- NBA All-Star
- All-NBA First Team
- AP Athlete of the Year
- *Sports Illustrated* Sportsperson of the Year

2014-2015 Season

- NBA All-Star
- All-NBA First Team

2013-2014 Season

- NBA All-Defensive Second Team
- NBA All-Star
- All-NBA First Team

2012-2013 Season

- NBA Champion
- NBA Finals MVP
- NBA MVP
- NBA All-Star
- AP Athlete of the Year
- NBA All-Defensive First Team
- All-NBA First Team

2011-2012 Season

- NBA Champion
- NBA Finals MVP
- NBA MVP
- NBA All-Star
- All-NBA First Team
- NBA All-Defensive First Team
- USA Basketball Male Athlete of the Year
- *Sporting News* Athlete of the Year
- Olympic Gold Medal

2010-2011 Season

- NBA All-Star
- All-NBA First Team
- NBA All-Defensive First Team

2009-2010 Season

- NBA MVP
- NBA All-Star
- All-NBA First Team
- NBA All-Defensive First Team

2008-2009 Season

- NBA MVP
- NBA All-Star
- All-NBA First Team
- NBA All-Defensive First Team

2007-2008 Season

- NBA All-Star
- NBA All-Star Game MVP
- All-NBA First Team
- NBA Scoring
- Olympic Gold Medal

2006-2007 Season

- NBA All-Star
- All-NBA Second Team

2005-2006 Season

- NBA All-Star
- NBA All-Star Game MVP
- All-NBA First Team
- FIBA World Championship Bronze Medal
- Sporting News NBA MVP

2004-2005 Season

- NBA All-Star
- All-NBA Second Team

2003-2004 Season

- NBA Rookie of the Year
- NBA All-Rookie First Team
- Olympic Bronze Medal

2002-2003 Season

- High School National Champion
- OHSAA Champion
- Gatorade National Player of the Year
- *USA Today* High School Player of the Year
- Ohio Mr. Basketball
- *USA Today* All-USA First Team
- PARADE High School Player of the Year
- Naismith Prep Player of the Year
- McDonald's National Player of the Year
- McDonald's High School All-American

- McDonald's All American Game Player
- EA Sports Roundball Classic MVP
- Jordan Capital Classic MVP

2001-2002 Season

- Gatorade National Player of the Year
- Ohio Mr. Basketball
- *USA Today* All-USA First Team
- PARADE High School Player of the Year

2000-2001 Season

- OHSAA Champion
- Ohio Mr. Basketball
- *USA Today* All-USA First Team

1999-2000

- OHSAA Champion

CHAPTER 16

NBA CAREER STATISTICS

Legend					
GP	Games played	GS	Games started	MPG	Minutes per game
FG%	Field goal percentage	3P%	3-point field goal percentage	FT%	Free throw percentage
RPG	Rebounds per game	APG	Assists per game	SPG	Steals per game
BPG	Blocks per game	PPG	Points per game	**Bold**	Career high

†	Denotes seasons in which James won an NBA championship
*	Led the league

Regular Season

Year	Team	GP	GS	MPG	FG%	3P%	FT%	RPG	APG	SPG	BPG	PPG
2003–04	Cleveland	79	79	39.5	.417	.290	.754	5.5	5.9	1.6	.7	20.9
2004–05	Cleveland	80	80	42.4*	.472	.351	.750	7.4	7.2	**2.2**	.7	27.2
2005–06	Cleveland	79	79	42.5	.480	.335	.738	7.0	6.6	1.6	.8	**31.4**
2006–07	Cleveland	78	78	40.9	.476	.319	.698	6.7	6.0	1.6	.7	27.3
2007–08	Cleveland	75	74	40.4	.484	.315	.712	7.9	7.2	1.8	**1.1**	30.0*
2008–09	Cleveland	81	81	37.7	.489	.344	**.780**	7.6	7.2	1.7	**1.1**	28.4
2009–10	Cleveland	76	76	39.0	.503	.333	.767	7.3	8.6	1.6	1.0	29.7
2010–11	Miami	79	79	38.8	.510	.330	.759	7.5	7.0	1.6	.6	26.7
2011–12†	Miami	62	62	37.5	.531	.362	.771	7.9	6.2	1.9	.8	27.1
2012–13†	Miami	76	76	37.9	.565	**.406**	.753	8.0	7.3	1.7	.9	26.8
2013–14	Miami	77	77	37.7	**.567**	.379	.750	6.9	6.4	1.6	.3	27.1
2014–15	Cleveland	69	69	36.1	.488	.354	.710	6.0	7.4	1.6	.7	25.3
2015–16†	Cleveland	76	76	35.6	.520	.309	.731	7.4	6.8	1.4	.6	25.3
2016–17	Cleveland	74	74	37.8*	.548	.363	.674	**8.6**	**8.7**	1.2	.6	26.4
Career		1061	1060	38.9	.501	.342	.740	7.3	7.0	1.6	.8	27.1
All-Star		13	13	29.4	.518	.344	.735	6.0	5.8	1.3	.2	24.2

Playoffs

Year	Team	GP	GS	MPG	FG%	3P%	FT%	RPG	APG	SPG	BPG	PPG
2006	Cleveland	13	13	46.5	.476	.333	.737	8.1	5.8	1.4	.7	30.8
2007	Cleveland	20	20	44.7	.416	.280	.755	8.1	8.0	1.7	.5	25.1
2008	Cleveland	13	13	42.5	.411	.257	.731	7.8	7.6	1.8	1.3	28.2
2009	Cleveland	14	14	41.4	.510	.333	.749	9.1	7.3	1.6	.9	35.3
2010	Cleveland	11	11	41.8	.502	.400	.733	9.3	7.6	1.7	1.8	29.1
2011	Miami	21	21	43.9	.466	.353	.763	8.4	5.9	1.7	1.2	23.7
2012†	Miami	23	23	42.7	.500	.259	.739	9.7	5.6	1.9	.7	30.3
2013†	Miami	23	23	41.7	.491	.375	.777	8.4	6.6	1.8	.8	25.9
2014	Miami	20	20	38.2	.565	.407	.806	7.1	4.8	1.9	.6	27.4
2015	Cleveland	20	20	42.2	.417	.227	.731	11.3	8.5	1.7	1.1	30.1
2016†	Cleveland	21	21	39.1	.525	.340	.661	9.5	7.6	2.3	1.3	26.3
2017	Cleveland	18	18	41.3	.565	.411	.698	9.1	7.8	1.9	1.3	32.8
Career		217	217	42.1	.485	.330	.742	8.9	6.9	1.8	1.0	28.4

CONLUSION

LeBron James is the type of athlete that comes along very rarely. Basketball fans of this generation should feel blessed to witness the evolution of such an extraordinary and versatile player.

He has grown from a young kid, erratic and somewhat ungrateful, to a poised athlete that will leave an immense impact on basketball, as well as the general social world, for decades to come. Although he is naturally gifted, strong, and coordinated, he has worked unquestionably hard day in and day out throughout his life to achieve the success that he has achieved today.

And the best part is, there is only more to come.

ABOUT THE AUTHOR

Steve James isn't your typical sports fan. While there are some that will always make time to watch the big game, James started following the NBA at a very young age and has watched some of the best players in the history of the NBA from the very beginning. Even at that young age, he started paying attention to who was really standing out on the court–greats like Michael Jordan, Magic Johnson or Larry Bird. Steve follows the game till this date and knows the ins and outs of the greatest NBA stars of today, like Kobe Bryant, LeBron James, Kevin Durant or Stephen Curry. Having carefully watched these players on the court and studied their lives, he has a unique perspective into their success, how it was achieved, and what makes them so great.

He has an insider view into the secrets that have made these players so successful. By collecting this information into his books, he hopes to help not just young, aspiring basketball players, but all people to learn the secrets of what it takes to be successful. By looking at how these players have reached their goals, the readers will glean the information they need to reach their own goals. Steve's years of analyzing play styles, successes, failures, training routines, etc. gives him a real insight into these players!

Made in the USA
San Bernardino, CA
15 January 2019